COUNTDOWN TO A VERY SPECIAL CHRISTMAS

Robert Peprah-Gyamfi

Kiddy Kiddy Books

Illustrated by: Jessica Otabil
Published by Kiddy Kiddy Books

www.kiddykiddybooks.com
email: info@kiddykiddybooks.com

ISBN: 978-1-913285-18-0

KIDDY KIDDY BOOKS SERIES NO. 2

COUNTDOWN TO A VERY SPECIAL CHRISTMAS

COUNTDOWN TO A VERY SPECIAL CHRISTMAS is part of the KIDDY KIDDY Books Series. The series follows the life of Kofi Mensah, a little boy growing up in Kookookrom, a tiny village in Ghana, West Africa.

CHAPTER 1

Let me tell you about Kofi Mensah. He is four years old. He lives in a little village in Ghana, in West Africa. The village is called Kookookrom which means Cocoa Settlement.

The name of their village can be translated as Cocoa Town, Cocoa Village or even Cocoa Settlement. In this book we shall stick with Cocoa Settlement.

Kofi is the third child of his parents. His father's name is Kwabena Baah; his mother is called Amma Dede. In Kofi's culture, women do not have to take the name of their husbands after marriage.

Kofi has two older brothers, Yaw Baako and Kwaku Manu. Yaw is nine years old. Kwaku is seven years old.

Kookookrom has a hot climate. Because of the hot climate, the residents usually go about in lightweight clothes. Like other children in the little village, Kofi usually walks around during the day wearing underpants with nothing on top.

Apart from his underpants, Kofi also possesses a piece of cotton cloth. The piece of cotton cloth is known as *ntama* in Kofi's Twi language. *Ntama* is also known as African wax print or African fabric.

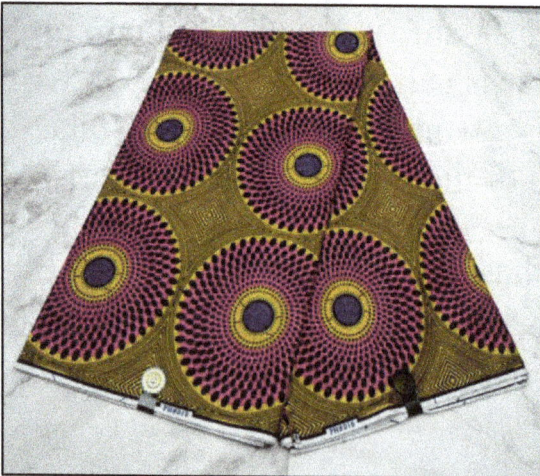

Kofi wears his ntama by wrapping it around his body. To prevent it from dropping off his body, he usually ties the two ends of the cloth into a knot around his neck. Kofi wears his cloth not only during the day, but also at night, as the same piece of cloth serves as cover for his body when he goes to sleep.

"Doesn't Kofi possess pyjamas or night clothes?" one may ask.

The answer is no. Indeed, apart from the two items of clothing just referred to, Kofi possesses no other clothing.

"What happens when Kofi's only two items of clothing become dirty and need washing? Does he have to go about naked while they are being cleaned?" one may ask.

No, Kofi does not have to go naked while his clothing is being washed. To ensure her little boy does not have to go about unclothed, Amma Dede came up with a plan.

This was her plan or strategy: after Kofi's clothes got dirty, she collected and handwashed Kofi's underpants just as he was about to go to sleep.

After washing the underpants, Kofi's mother hung them on the washing line and left them to dry during the night. As already mentioned, Kofi lives in a warm climate. Usually by the time he woke up the following morning, the underpants were dry and ready to be worn.

After Kofi had put on his underpants, his mother collected his dirty piece of cloth, washed it and left it in the sun to dry. Kofi was left to walk around without any top as he waited for the cloth to dry.

Thanks to the good African weather, Kofi's piece of cloth dried after a short while. Soon, Kofi could be seen wearing both items of clothing-- clean and good-looking. When after a while both items of clothing got dirty, Kofi's mother repeated the routine.

As already mentioned, Kofi is four years old. Since he was old enough to understand his environment, Kofi has known no other items of clothing apart from the two already referred to.

* * *

Kofi's ntama, or piece of cotton cloth, meanwhile was worn out and torn in several places. One day he went out to play with Abenaa, his favourite playmate.

Abenaa is the daughter of their immediate neighbour. Both families are good friends. Kofi returned home after a while in tears.

"Why are you weeping, my dear?" his mother asked, very worried.

"Abenaa has been nasty to me!" Kofi replied, wiping the tears from his eyes.

"Tell me, what happened?" Amma Dede enquired.

"As we were playing, an argument developed between us: 'Shut up, silly boy! How dare you behave so rudely towards me, the pretty little Princess of Kookookrom! You'd rather ask your poor parents to replace your torn and stinking clothes than dare challenge me!' she shouted at me."

"Did she really say that?"

"Yes, mother; she said exactly that!"

"Don't be sad, my dear. Leave the matter with me. I will have a conversation with her parents. They'd better teach their daughter good manners so she does not go about insulting other people's children."

There followed a short silence. Soon Kofi began to speak again.

"Mama, I think Abenaa is right!" he pointed out.

"If you think she is right, then why are you complaining?"

"I am not complaining. I am only saddened I have to wear tatty clothes."

"It is really unfortunate that you have to go about with worn-out clothes. You should bear in mind however that you are not the only one in the family going about in shabby clothes. Everyone else —your two elder brothers, your father and myself—has to do the same."

"I don't care what others are wearing. I want my clothes replaced. So please tell me, Mama, when are you going to replace them?"

"You'd better ask your father."

"Why should I ask father? Why can't you answer?"

"Well, if you are insisting on an answer, it is the following—you will get a new piece of cloth to replace the old one at Christmas."

"Christmas? What is Christmas, Mama?" Kofi enquired.

"Hey, Kofi! Don't you know what Christmas is?" shouted Yaw who had been following the conversation.

"Hey, Yaw, stay out of the matter! I am talking to Mama. You'd better not interfere."

"I am not interfering in anything." Yaw began. "I am only surprised you have forgotten all about Christmas. We celebrated Christmas not very long ago."

"Really? When was that?" Kofi asked, surprised.

"Hey, Mama, what is wrong with your little son? He has forgotten all about the last Christmas. I remember how happy he was when I presented him with a piece of biscuit I received from our Sunday School teacher." Yaw stated.

"Don't be surprised, Yaw, that your little brother has forgotten all about last Christmas. He was only a little over three years old at the time."

"I find it very strange!" said Yaw.

"Yaw, you should bear in mind that babies and little children tend to forget easily."

"Did I also forget so quickly when I was a baby?"

"I don't want to answer the question for you. Instead I will narrate an incident that happened when you were young. When I finish, let me know if you still remember it."

"Okay, go ahead."

"When you were two-and-a-half-years old, you fell seriously ill. Due to lack of money, we kept you at home for a while, hoping you would get better. No, that was not the case. Your condition worsened instead of improving.

In the end we took you to the Makokrom Hospital, which is thirty kilometres (twenty miles) away. On our arrival two friendly nurse attended to you. Just as they were checking on you, all of sudden, you began to urinate! The fountain of water coming from your body went straight into the face of one of the nurses!"

"No, no! That was not me! How could I do that?" Yaw protested.

"That is exactly what happened, my dear!" Amma Dede pointed out.

"What a shame! I have no memory of it!"

"Well, you can now understand Kofi if he tells you he has no recollection of last Christmas. It takes a while before young children are able to remember things that happen to them."

"How long?" Yaw enquired.

"My father told me it is only after children have attained the age of four years that they are able to keep things in their mind."

"Oh, I see!"

* * *

Amma Dede thought Kofi would leave the matter of Christmas to rest. No, he didn't!

"Mama, you are yet to answer my question." Kofi turned to her.

"What question?"

"I asked you to explain Christmas to me, have you also forgotten?"

"Okay, I will explain now, so pay attention. Christmas is a festival to mark the birth of Baby Jesus in a little town called Bethlehem many years ago."

"Baby Jesus?"

"Yes."

"Who is Baby Jesus?"

"He is a friend of children."

"A friend of children?"

"Yes. He was born in Bethlehem."

"Baby Jesus was born in Bethlehem?"

"Yes."

"Where is Bethlehem?"

"I have no idea, darling. Our Pastor mentioned the matter in church. I just accepted it without question."

Amma Dede, thought her little boy would finally leave the matter of Christmas to rest! No, he wouldn't.

After a short silence he turned to his mother again and asked:

"Mama, is Bethlehem far from Kookookrom?"

"I told you, I have no idea where it is located. One thing I am certain though: it is nowhere near Kookookrom."

At that juncture, Kofi turned to his father, who had just returned home from working in the fields.

"Papa, where exactly is Bethlehem located?"

"No idea, my dear. I will ask our Pastor." Kofi's father replied.

"Please do that. I would like to travel to Bethlehem, to pay a visit to Baby Jesus! Mother tells me he is a friend of children."

"Okay, my dear. In the meantime, please leave me alone to rest. I am tired from working in the fields."

Kofi left his father at peace. Not so his mother. Turning to her, he continued:

"Mama, I still don't understand."

"What don't you understand?"

"You mentioned that Christmas celebrates the birth of Baby Jesus in Bethlehem. What has that got to do with my tatty clothes? Why do I have to wait till Christmas to have it replaced? Why can't it be done straightaway?"

Amma Dede thought of the best way to explain the matter to Kofi so he would leave her in peace. Quickly she thought of an explanation:

"Kofi, pay attention as I explain to you why we are asking you to wait till Christmas to replace your tatty clothes," she began.

"It is indeed the desire of your Papa and myself that you go about in good clothes. Papa and myself are really embarrassed to see you and your brothers going about in such appalling clothes.

We have a problem though—the problem of money. One needs money to purchase anything, including your clothes. We cannot just take you to a shop and ask the seller to hand us new clothes to present to you. The owner will only be prepared to do so in exchange for money. So we need to earn the money required to purchase the clothes. Unfortunately we are short of money most of the time.

The only means by which we earn money is through the sale of the cocoa beans we harvest from our farm. By chance, we usually harvest our cocoa beans not long before Christmas.

Since Christmas is generally associated with giving presents and gifts, it has become a custom for everyone in the village, including ourselves, to wait until Christmas to replace the old clothes of our children. Even though we could replace your clothes from the money from the sale of our cocoa beans a few weeks before Christmas, we wait until Christmas to do so."

"So I have to wait till Christmas to receive new clothes?"

"Yes, my dear!"

"Are you sure you will earn enough money from this year's cocoa harvest to permit you to buy us new clothes?"

"Yes, indeed. I visited our cocoa farm not long ago. The majority of the trees are bearing abundant fruits. We are sure to have a good harvest, which will enable us to replace your clothes as promised."

"What happens if the harvest turns out to be poor?"

"In that case, everyone will have to do without new clothes at Christmas. That is exactly what happened last year. We couldn't replace your clothes. That explains why your ntama is in such a sore state—you have been wearing it for more than a year and a half!"

"Do you also have to wait till Christmas for replacement of your worn-out clothes?"

"Yes, indeed. Your father and I put the interests of our children ahead of us. We buy new clothes for ourselves only after we have been able to meet your needs."

"That is very kind of you, Mother," Kofi declared.

There followed a short silence, to be broken by Kofi.

"I have another question, Mama."

"My goodness, I am tired of your questions."

"This will certainly be my last."

"Sure?"

"Yes, I promise."

"Okay, go ahead."

"How long do we have to wait till Christmas?"

"Okay, pay attention as I explain. December 25 is Christmas Day. We are now in the middle of September. September will be followed by October. October for its part will be followed by November. After November comes finally December, the "Christmas month!" Even after entering December, we have to wait twenty-five days till Christmas!"

"So how many days are left before Christmas?"

"Hey, my dear, I thought you had already asked your final question!"

"My apologies, Mama, please answer me this one last time!"

"Much as I would have loved to have answered that question, I am afraid I am not in a position to do so. I did not have the opportunity to attend school so I don't know how to add up the figures. You may try your luck with your father."

"No, I promised not to disturb him. I am grateful for the information you have so far provided. I cannot just wait for the arrival of Christmas—yes for the opportunity to get a replacement for my shabby clothes."

* * *

The other members of Kofi's family could only wish the conversation they had with him concerning the coming of Christmas had not taken place! It was too late for them to change anything though!

From that very day on, almost everything Kofi said or did had something to do with the coming Christmas and the new ntama he had been promised to replace his old one.

It all began the very next day after his conversation with his parents concerning the advent of Christmas. Usually, the first thought that came into his mind on waking up from bed was food. He would usually approach his mother and begin:

"Mama, I am hungry. When will breakfast be ready?"

That indeed was the question Amma Dede expected from him when he woke up the next day. To her amazement Kofi turned to her and began:

"Mama, what day is it today?"

"Saturday," she answered, "why do you want to know?"

"I thought today was Christmas!"

"No, my dear! I made that clear to you yesterday! You will have to wait till 25 December, which is about three months away."

"Three months away! Is there no way of bringing the date forward?"

"No, darling. You'll just have to exercise patience," his mother urged him.

"Oh dear. Christmas, are you not able to visit us earlier than scheduled?" Kofi murmured to himself as he walked away from his mother, disappointment written in his face.

* * *

Kofi's irritating questions to other members of the family as to when Christmas would arrive turned out to be an almost daily occurrence. If only the other members of Kofi's family could do anything to escape his endless queries and references to the coming Christmas and the joy of getting a replacement for his clothes! Of course they could not.

After being bombarded day after day with Kofi's references to Christmas, one evening as the family gathered for their evening meal, Yaw began:

"Hello, Everyone. May I please have your attention."

"What is the matter?" his father wanted to know.

"Well, I have decided with effect from today to change the name of the youngest member of our family from Kofi Mensah to Kofi Buronya! (Buronya is the Twi word for Christmas. So, all hail Kofi Buronya, the youngest member of our family!"

"How dare you change my name without my permission!" Kofi protested.

Despite Kofi's protests, soon everyone at home was calling him Kofi Buronya!

CHAPTER 2

As already stated, cocoa was Kofi's parents' main source of income, and the same was true for other members of the small community..

Starting from the beginning of October, the residents of the village, including Kofi's parents, began harvesting their cocoa.

Apart from Kofi, who was considered too young to take part in the harvesting, all the other members of the family became involved in the process.

First Kofi's father cut down the pods growing on the trees with the help of a machete.

The other members of the family
gathered the pods together at a central
collecting point on the farm. Next, the
pods were cut open with a machete.
Each pod contained 30 to 50 large seeds
or beans surrounded by a white pulp.
Kofi and other family members removed
the beans from the pods and gathered
them together into a heap. The heap was
covered with broad leaves of the banana
plant and left in the field for five to
seven days to undergo fermentation.

After a period of fermentation, the beans
were then carried home and spread on

specially prepared mats to dry over a period of about fourteen days.

The dried beans were finally collected into sacks and sold at a cocoa-purchasing outpost in the village.

Usually Kofi's father received payment for his cocoa beans the next day after they had been sold. As Kofi's father prepared to leave home the next day to visit the purchasing agent to claim the money from the sales of his produce, Kofi turned to him and began:

"Papa, may I come along?"

"Why do you want to accompany me?"

"To ensure thieves do not snatch the money from you!"

"Can you repeat what you said?" said Kwabena Baah, his father. He could hardly believe what he was hearing!

"I want to accompany you to collect the money to ensure thieves do not rob you of the money!" Kofi stressed.

"Kofi, you big mouth! What strength do you have to prevent that from happening?" Yaw remarked.

"You wait and see! In any case, I want to accompany Papa, to ensure we get the money home safely. If thieves do make away with the money, he will not be able to replace my worn-out clothes."

At that stage Kofi's father turned to the rest of the family:

"Well, folks. Let's allow him to go with me—if only to prevent him from becoming too disappointed."

So Kofi accompanied his father to the cocoa-purchasing agent.

"I have brought my security guard," Kofi's father joked as they took their seat in front of the purchasing agent.

"Indeed?"

"Yes, he insisted on coming along, to prevent thieves from stealing the money from me!"

"That is a really brave young boy! We could offer him full-time employment here as a security guard!" the agent joked.

Kofi was wide-eyed as he watched the agent count out the notes.

After Kofi's Papa had placed the notes
into a bag and sealed it, he said goodbye
to the agent and left the room, Kofi
walking close by his side.

Hardly had both arrived home than Kofi turned to his father and began:

"Papa, we now have money in abundance. Can you please replace my old clothes straightaway?"

At that juncture, Amma Dede, intervened.

"Kofi, have you forgotten the conversation I had with you not long ago, in which I pointed out to you that it has become a custom to wait until Christmas before handing out such presents?"

"Yes, I remember, but I am scared about what Abenaa told me."

"What did she tell you?"

"She told me, my present piece of cotton cloth is so tired being worn on a daily basis, it will one day speak to me, yes, beg me to give it some rest!"

"Hey, Kofi, do not believe what that girl tells you. You are the same age as her. Do not allow her to behave as if she were your boss," Yaw cautioned his little brother.

"Abenaa is indeed a bossy little girl. She'd better look for someone else to rule over—not my little son!" Kofi's mother added.

CHAPTER 3

18 December – a week to go until Christmas!

Kofi's long wait for the arrival of the big day was gradually drawing to a close—only seven days left to go! There was much activity in the whole village. Not only Kofi's parents, but all the residents of the whole village were occupied with the preparation towards the big day.

Kookookrom is a farming community and usually residents visit their farms every day of the week apart from Sundays. The only exception is the period between Christmas and the New Year. It has indeed become a tradition for the residents to stay away from working in the fields starting from Christmas Day till the day after the New Year. Because of that, residents were taking steps to build up sufficient stocks of food to take them through the rest period.

As far as Kofi was concerned, what mattered most was not the stock of food his parents were building up, but rather the promised replacement of his old *ntama*. The piece of cotton cloth was in the meantime a real eyesore—it was displaying tears of various sizes all over.

Before he retired to bed that evening, an idea occurred to him to count the number of torn spots on his *ntama*. One, two, three, four, five, six, seven… That was how far he could go. Yaw was teaching him how to count; he hoped to build on his counting skills with time.

Though his parents had already advised him not to believe Abenaa's lie that his *ntama* could one day acquire a voice and speak out in protest against being overused, somehow Kofi could not completely disbelieve her.

* * *

19 December

Kofi's parents had purchased a large piece of *ntama* for the children at Christmas.

Kofi's parents wanted to surprise their children at Christmas with the new piece of cotton cloth. They therefore handed it over to Tailor Ayigbe without first showing it to their boys.

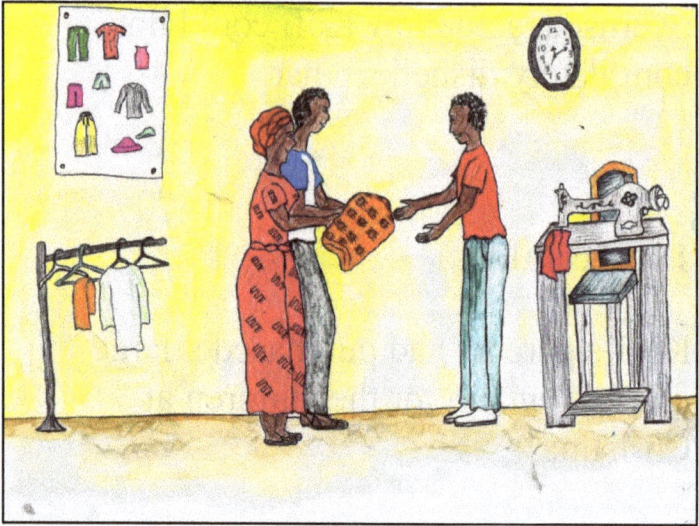

Tailor Ayigbe was a well-loved resident of the little village. He was the only tailor in the village. Every resident of the village went to him to get their clothes sewn.

20 December

Tailor Ayigbe arrived at Kofi's home, a measuring tape in his hand.

"Hey, boys, come forward. I want to take your measurements. I need your respective heights as well as your waist measurements."

Kofi's two elder brothers, already familiar with the ritual from previous years, heeded the call without asking questions.

Kofi on his part was experiencing the occasion for the first time and wouldn't comply without understanding what it was all about. The beloved tailor of the village took time to explain the purpose of his visit to the understanding of the inquisitive four-year-old.

Just as he put the assignment behind him and prepared to leave for his shop, Kofi turned to him and began:

"Where then is the piece of *ntama* you are sewing for me?"

"It is in my shop."

"Should I come along and have a look?"

"No."

"Why not?"

"I am under instructions from your parents not to allow any one of you to have a look until they are presented to you by your parents."

Though not very convinced, Kofi did not ask any further questions.

21 December

Kofi's father visited the market at Mangokrom, a little town two miles (three kilometres) away from Kookookrom. He returned with a big rooster in his hand.

"Papa, what are you going to do with the chicken?" Kofi enquired.

"It will be used to prepare our Christmas meal," was the answer.

"Will it be served alive?" Kofi asked.

"Hey, Kofi, how can anyone consume a living bird!" Kwaku his brother who was born immediately before him remarked.

"Papa said it will be used to prepare the Christmas meal. How will that happen?"

"You can find out from your mother," Kofi's father advised.

"Hey, Mama. How will this chicken end up being part of the Christmas meal?"

"You would not understand if I explain it to you. You must be patient. When the time comes, I will invite you to be around, to observe me from beginning to the very end."

22 December

Kofi's parents and his two elder brothers were visiting the fields to harvest food for the family. When Kofi was a baby, his mother carried him wrapped to her back when visiting the farm. Later, when he grew too big to be carried on her back, Kofi's father carried him around his neck. Kofi was now capable of walking to the farm himself. Kofi could only walk very slowly. Because of this, Kofi parents decided on this occasion not to take him to the fields. They needed to walk very briskly to the farm. Their plan was to make two trips to the farm to fetch as much food as possible for Christmas.

Fortunately for them, their neighbours, Abenaa's parents, had decided to stay home from working in the fields that day. They agreed to take care of Kofi while the rest of his family worked in the fields.

Kofi was delighted at the opportunity to play with Abenaa. His hope was that both of them would tolerate each other throughout the time they were playing together. This was not always the case; there had indeed been instances when the joy of playing together had ended in misunderstanding, argument and in rare instances, even a fight!

23 December

Kofi had been told prior to going to bed the previous night that Christmas was only three days away. Yet on waking up he headed straight for his mother and began:

"Mama, is today Christmas?"

"No, my dear, Still two days to go!" Amma Dede replied.

Looking disappointed, Kofi left her alone and went out to play with 'Poor no friend', the family cat.

At breakfast-time, Yaw turned to their Papa and began:

"Papa, are we not going to put up a Christmas tree?

"I am too occupied with other matters to think about a Christmas tree," came the reply.

"Papa, what is a Christmas tree?" Kofi enquired.

"Yaw explain to your brother what a Christmas tree is—as you brought up the topic."

"Ach, Papa, how can I explain a Christmas tree to Kofi's understanding without showing him one! So please help us put one up."

For a while, Kofi's father resisted the idea of going into the woods to fetch a Christmas tree. After his boys kept on pleading with him, he had a change of mind.

"Okay, you've persuaded me. I will help you put up a Christmas tree!"

Saying that he got out of his seat and fetched a machete.

Next he turned to his two older children and began:

"Yaw and Kwaku, you are coming along with me, aren't you?"

"Yes, Papa!" both shouted aloud as if with a single voice.

Moments later the three of them were heading for the woods bordering on the compound of their home.

"I want to come along!" Kofi cried aloud, running after them as he did.

"No, stay with your mother! You are too young for this assignment," his father urged him.

"Please!"

"No!" his father insisted.

Reluctantly, Kofi returned to his seat.

The three returned after a while. Kwabena Baah, their Papa, was carrying in both hands a young oil palm tree. It was about twenty inches (half a metre) tall.

Kofi was surprised at the sight of the uprooted palm tree in his father's hands.

"What are you going to do with the young palm tree, Papa?" he enquired.

"We told you we were going to fetch a Christmas tree, didn't we?"

"Yes, you did. I didn't expect a palm tree though!"

"What else did you expect?"

"I thought it was a special tree sent by Baby Jesus, not a young palm tree!"

"A special tree sent by Baby Jesus? Are you daydreaming, Kofi?" Yaw retorted.

"Keep yourself out of it, Yaw, " Kofi protested. "It is Papa I am talking with and not yourself."

"Calm down, Kofi, and pay attention as I try to explain." Kwabena Baah urged his youngest child.

"It is a tradition in Kookookrom and the rest of Ghana to set up a young palm tree as a Christmas tree."

"So we destroy a whole young palm tree just for the sake of putting up a Christmas tree, don't we?"

"No, we don't."

"Yes, we do!"

"I realise you are a very caring boy, Kofi. You even concern yourself with the welfare of plants. I do also."

"If you do, why then did you destroy the young palm tree?"

"No, I didn't. To make sure the young tree is not destroyed, I took time to remove it carefully from the ground with all its roots and the surrounding soil. I will return it to the very spot where I took it from when Christmas is over."

"Sure?"

"Yes, indeed."

Next Kofi's father carefully placed the young palm tree on the ground. He then collected a plant pot from their garden, filled it with soil and planted the young palm tree in it.

"Hey, everyone, our Christmas tree is ready!" he announced.

"Not really, Papa!" said Yaw.

"What do you mean?" his father asked.

"We are yet to decorate it!"

"Decorate our Christmas tree?" Kofi enquired, very surprised at the idea.

"Yes, indeed." Yaw replied.

After a short silence, Yaw turned to their Papa:

"Papa, please, have you got some money to spare?"

"What for?" he enquired.

"To purchase a few items to decorate our Christmas tree."

In response, Kwabena Baah, placed his hands into his pocket, pulled out his wallet, unzipped it, pulled out a few coins and dropped them into Yaw's outstretched palm.

Moments later, Yaw was running out of the house, heading for the small grocery shop in the centre of the village—the only of its kind in the little settlement of Kookookrom.

He returned a few minutes later with a few packets in his hands. Opening the packets, he went about hanging the ornaments carefully on the branches of the young oil palm tree. Yaw took about half an hour to decorate the Christmas tree. Finally, he declared at the top of his voice:

"Hello, everyone, pay attention! I have the honour of presenting to you this year's Christmas tree!"

The announcement was greeted with a clap of the hands by the rest of the family.

24 December

On waking up, Kofi somehow thought the much-awaited day had arrived. To his disappointment he was told he had to sleep for yet another night.

"Should I return to bed straight away and sleep till tomorrow?" Kofi suggested.

"That is crazy idea, Kofi!" Yaw stated.

"Why?" Kofi enquired.

"We have to live through today. That means we have to get up and go through our usual activities. If you go to bed now, you will be so hungry you might die of hunger!"

"Mama, can one really die of hunger?"

"Yes, indeed, if one stops eating for a while, one can indeed die of hunger."

* * *

Kofi's parents spent much of the day making the final preparation towards the arrival of Christmas.

The day is over. Darkness, deep darkness, has returned to the village. There is no electricity in the village. The residents have to resort to kerosene lanterns and lamps.

It is late in the night. Kofi's family has retired to bed. Everyone is lost in sleep— not so Kofi! Poor Kofi, much as he wanted to sleep, he could not close his eyes to sleep. Kofi wondered why he could not close his eyes and get to sleep. Usually he was a good sleeper; but not on this occasion though.

As he lay in bed tossing and turning in bed, unable to sleep, Kofi began to wonder why he could not sleep. Was it due to the excitement? Was it because he was unable to free his mind of the tension that had built up in his mind concerning the new clothes he was expecting to receive on Christmas Day? Fortunately, somehow, Kofi managed to get to sleep at last, enabling him to regenerate the much-needed energy to face the much-awaited day.

25 December

Christmas Day!

At long last the day Kofi had been yearning for had arrived!

On waking up, Kofi hurried to his parents to demand his Christmas clothes.

What a strange scene met his eyes! Instead of the happy and joyous faces he had expected from his parents, he met both of them grieving. Indeed, his mother was not only grieving, she was crying at the top of her voice, with tears dropping freely from her eyes.

"Mama, Papa, what is wrong with you? Are you in pain?" Kofi enquired, very surprised indeed.

Instead of getting an answer, his parents ignored him and kept on weeping.

Kofi thought it was only his parents who were grieving. That turned out not to be the case. Indeed, from every direction of the village, he heard cries and screams.

Who should Kofi turn to for an explanation of the strange things happening around him? In the end he decided to find out from his brothers.

"Kwaku, do you have any idea as to what is wrong with Mama and Papa?" he began.

"They are weeping for our loved ones who passed away in the course of the year gone by"

"Why should they do so on Christmas Day, the day that is meant to be a day of joy and merrymaking?

"That is exactly the question I put to Mama the first time I experienced the scene. That was two years ago."

"We are mourning our loved ones who have passed away and are unable to join us for the Christmas festivities," she explained.

"I find it very strange!" Kofi remarked.

"Well, I suggest you question Mama on the matter yourself, she has ceased crying. Maybe she is now in a position to explain to you."

Kofi did as requested.

"Mama, Kwaku tells me you are weeping for those of our relations who did not make it to this Christmas. Is that really the case?"

"Yes, it is."

"Will your weeping help and persuade them to come back to life?"

"No."

"Why not?"

"I don't think you will understand even if I explain, so let us leave the matter as it is."

After a while, not only Kofi's parents, but the whole community stopped grieving and went about their normal activities.

Kofi's mother cooked a tasty meal of boiled rice, served with fried vegetables and beef sauce. Rice and beef did not belong on the daily menu of Kofi's family. Kofi's parents could hardly afford any food item not grown by themselves. Indeed, it was the first time in the whole year that such a meal was being served by Kofi's mother.

After eating until he was full, Kofi turned to Kwaku and began:

"That was indeed very rich food."

"You be patient and wait until tomorrow!"

"What do you mean?"

"Well, when I was as young as yourself, I was also fascinated with the meal served on Christmas Day. As it became clear to me later, it is on 26 December, Boxing Day, that the main Christmas meal is served. When I asked mother for the reason, she explained to me that Christmas Day was the day of remembering the departed ones, those who could not make it to Christmas. It was thus not appropriate to cook the best meal of the season on that day. Instead, such a meal was reserved for 26 December."

Kofi returned to bed with mixed feelings. On the one hand he was disappointed he had not been presented with his much-awaited Christmas clothes. He drew consolation from the fact that he needed to sleep only one more night for the dawn of the much-awaited day.

26 December

Finally, 26 December arrived, the day Kofi was to be presented with his new ntama.

After breakfast, Kwabena Baah, left for the sleeping room. He returned a short while later holding a bag. After taking his seat he began:

"Now, at last, the time has come for you to receive your Christmas clothes. Happily, this year, Amma and myself have managed to purchase new clothes to replace your old ones. We cannot promise you new clothes next Christmas. For this Christmas, however, every one of you should rejoice at the fact that it has been possible for us to do so."

There was joyful expectation in the eyes of all the three boys as they waited to have a glimpse of their much-awaited Christmas clothes.

Next, their father unzipped the bag. Beginning with the youngest child, he handed each of the three their Christmas present, cut to their size by the well-loved Tailor Ayigbe.

Hurriedly, each of them dropped their old *ntama* off their body and put on the new one.

"It looks so beautiful. I like the colours!" Yaw remarked.

"Me too!" Kwaku added

"Papa, I have a question.," came the voice of the youngest member of the family.

"Kofi always has a question to ask!" Amma Dede joked.

"Okay, go ahead with your question, I am listening." Kwabena Baah urged his youngest son.

"Why is it that you presented each one of us with the same type of *ntama*?"

"Kofi, before I answer the question, I want to ask you a question." Kofi's father began.

"Let us suppose, I gave each one of you a different type of *ntama* and, when you took a look at Yaw's cloth, you found it nicer than yours. You would have asked us to give you Yaw's cloth instead, but you would have been told it was too late, you had to keep your own. How would you feel?"

"Very angry, really angry!"

"Now you have answered the question yourself. The main reason we decided to present all of you with the same type of *ntama* is to prevent discontent amongst you. We also did not want any one of you to accuse us of favouritism."

"Favouritism? What does that mean?"

"It means treating one person better than the other."

"Okay, I get it."

* * *

Kofi's face beamed with smiles as he tried to wrap his new piece of cloth around his body. For a while he struggled to wear it properly. Amma Dede, noticing the problem facing her little son, went to his assistance.

Hardly had Amma Dede helped Kofi put on his *ntama,* than he hurried out of the house.

"Hey, Kofi, where are you heading?" the other members of the family cried after him.

"I want to show Abenaa my new *ntama!*" he shouted back. Soon he disappeared out of sight.

Kofi and his favourite playmate, Abenaa! A kind of love–hate relationship had developed between them. One moment they seemed to be the very best of friends, playing and sharing things together; the next moment they would be at logger heads, insulting and behaving rudely towards each another.

The reaction of Abenaa towards Kofi, when he arrived at her home to show her his new cotton cloth, was not what Kofi had expected.

On his arrival, Kofi approached her, beaming with joy and began:

"Hello, Abenaa, have a look at my new Christmas cloth! Isn't it pretty!" he began.

Instead of the appreciation he expected from her, Abenaa rather looked at him scornfully and began:

"Kofi, don't think you have received the best Christmas cloth in the world! You just take a seat and wait. I will soon show you what I received from my lovely parents!"

Saying that, she disappeared into her room.

She returned a short while later in her Christmas clothes.

As already mentioned, it was the practice for the boys to wrap a single piece of *ntama* around their body.

The situation was different with girls. Their cloth was made of two parts: a top and a bottom.

Making use of the same material, a blouse or shirt (also known locally as *kaba)* was sewn to the size of the individual, up to the level of the navel or belly button.

After putting on the *kaba* to cover their top half, girls wrap a piece of the same material, cut to their size, around their lower body, from the waist down to the middle of their legs.

Abenaa's parents had selected a brilliant and delightfully coloured African print fabric for their daughter that Christmas.

Unlike Kofi, who had to go about barefooted, her parents had also presented her with a new pair of shoes to go with her gorgeous dress.

"Kofi, you came out proudly to show me you new clothes. Now you have a look at mine! Your outfit, for sure is no match for mine!"

Next Abenaa directed a scornful look towards Kofi's feet and began:

"Tell me, Kofi, where is the pair of sandals or shoes to match your clothes?"

Kofi felt upset by the unfriendly comments from his playmate. Everyone had been talking about being friendly to each other during the Christmas season. He expected Abenaa to treat him in a friendly manner by appreciating his clothes. Instead of doing that, she chose instead to highlight his shortcomings.

Kofi resolved not to play tit-for-tat with his playmate by passing any negative comment about her dress. Instead, he decided to be friendly to her and compliment her amazing outfit. She indeed looked charming and attractive in her Christmas dress!

"You look so lovely in your dress, Abenaa."

"Thank you very much, Kofi. I would however have preferred you said something like this: 'You look lovely and pretty in your gorgeous dress, my dear little Princess of Kookookrom!'"

Kofi could take no more of the boasting from his playmate.

"Okay, Abenaa, I must go now. See you later!"

"Call me 'Lovely Princess Abenaa!'"

"Okay, Lovely Princess Abenaa. I am on my way home!"

* * *

On reaching home, Kofi turned to his mother and began:

"Mama, Abenaa showed me a beautiful pair of shoes she received at Christmas to go with her gorgeous dress."

"Oh, did she!"

"Yes. Why didn't I receive a pair of shoes, just like Abenaa?"

"Kofi, don't compare yourself with Abenaa!"

"What do you mean by 'Don't compare yourself with Abenaa'?"

"I meant, don't try to be like Abenaa. You are two different individuals. You are called Kofi Mensah. She is called Abenaa Foriwaah!"

"Not 'Abenaa Foriwaah'!" Kofi attempted to correct his mother.

"What do you mean by that?" Amma Dede wondered.

"She asked me to call her 'Lovely Princess Abenaa'!"

"Who gave her that name?"

"Well, that is what she told me!"

"You may choose to call her by whichever name you prefer. I will call her Abenaa Foriwaah as that is what everyone, including her parents, call her!"

"Okay, let's leave the matter of the correct way to call Abenaa aside. Let's return to the issue of the shoes. Abenaa showed me her beautiful pair of shoes. I just want to know when I can expect my own pair of shoes, just like Abenaa?"

"Kofi, I want to ask you a question: Have you seen Yaw and Kwaku wearing any footwear?"

"No."

"How, can you expect your own footwear when your older brothers don't have their own?"

"Okay, you just visit the market and purchase a pair of shoes for each of us!"

"Things are not as easy as you think."

"Why not?"

"Have you forgotten the conversation I had with you not very long ago?"

"Which conversation?"

"That we require money to purchase such items!"

"But we have a lot of money at home!"

"Really?"

"Yes, indeed. I accompanied Papa the other day to collect a lot of money from the cocoa-purchasing agent. He could have used part of it to purchase shoes for all of us!"

"You collected lot of money with your father! Darling, take it from me: that was nothing at all! Indeed the money we earned from this year's cocoa harvest was just enough to purchase new clothes for you and your brothers. Your father and I were left with nothing!"

"Really?"

"Yes, that is the truth."

"Do you want part of my cloth? I am happy to share it with you!"

"That is very kind of you. No, you keep it for yourself. I am praying and hoping for a better cocoa harvest next year, which will enable us purchase not only African wax print for our children, but also a pair of shoes for each one of them!"

"And new clothes for yourself and Papa."

"Thank you for your kind thoughts and wishes. It is much appreciated."

* * *

It was not only Kofi who was keen to show his new clothes to the rest of the world! Every child in the village who was big enough and in good health came out on the main street of the little village to show off their new Christmas clothes or dress.

It was easy for a stranger visiting Kofi's village to make out which of the children walking along the street were siblings.

How could they know, one may ask?

The answer is that it was not only Kofi's parents who presented their three boys with the same type of *ntama* for Christmas to avoid being accused of bias. Almost every parent in the village did the same.

Kofi joined other children from the village on a walk along the main road. The aim of every one of them was to let the rest of the world have a look at their respective Christmas clothes.

After walking up and down the main road of the village for a while, Kofi joined his big brothers and other peers to attend the little village church.

In the church, Kofi could hardly concentrate enough to listen to the sermon. Pastor Kofi Poku, also known by everyone in the village as Papa Teacher, repeated what Kofi had already heard from his parents—that Christmas marks the birth of Baby Jesus in Bethlehem. Kofi was surprised to hear their Pastor mention that, at the birth of Baby Jesus, angels appeared from heaven to speak to shepherds looking after their sheep.

On hearing their Pastor speak of angels descending from heaven, Kofi turned to Yaw who was sitting near him and asked in quite a loud voice: "Yaw, what are angels?"

"Sssh, keep quiet boy and don't disturb the church!" an elderly woman sitting behind him urged him.

Kofi was not happy with the intervention of the stranger, yet he kept quiet.

Kofi was delighted when the church service came to an end. He had only managed to pay attention during the first few minutes of the sermon. For the rest of the time, his attention was far away from the church. Indeed, all his thoughts were about the tasty meal his mother was preparing. To be able to get the festive meal ready for everyone, Kofi's mother had decided to stay away from church that day.

On stepping out of the church building, Kofi turned to his brothers and began:

"Hey Yaw! Hey Kwaku! Hurry up! Let's get back home quickly to enjoy the Christmas meal."

"Kofi the foodie!" Yaw mocked him. "Stop thinking about food for now! Come along with us."

"Where to?"

"We are going round the village singing Christmas carols!"

"No, I am not coming! I am going back home for the chicken meal!" he insisted.

"The chicken meal will not be ready until late in the evening, my friend! If you don't come along, you will miss out on the tasty biscuits we are expecting to receive from residents of the homes we will be visiting."

Kofi was confused. What was he to do? Go home straightaway and wait till the Christmas meal was ready or join his brothers in singing the Christmas songs? In the end, he decided to join the others.

There was a total of twelve boys and girls in the group. Kofi spotted Abenaa amongst them. On this occasion, he did not want to be near her in the group. Why didn't he want to be close to his best friend and playmate, one would wonder? The answer is that he feared she would make fun of him if he was not able to sing the songs properly.

Yaw Baako, Kofi's eldest brother, who happen to be the oldest among the group, declared himself the team leader.

"Keep quiet, everyone!" Yaw called for order. "We are going to form two lines; the girls in front, the small boys should stand just behind the girls, and the big boys should stay at the very back of the line. Has everyone understood?"

After initial confusion, Yaw finally succeeded in getting the team to form two orderly lines.

"Now, everyone, we are going to learn a song." Yaw announced.

"Which song?" a little girl standing just near him enquired.

Yaw began singing the popular Ghanaian Christmas carol:

Buronya aba,
Afepa ato yen,
Yema mo afe nhyia pa!

(Christmas is here with us; we wish you a Merry Christmas)

"Raise your hands, those of you who are familiar with the song!" Yaw addressed the group.

Everyone present, apart from Kofi, put up their hands. On realising he was the only one in the group with his hand down, Kofi murmured to himself: "I don't want to be the odd one out!" Moments later his hand was also in the air.

"Hey, Kofi, when did you learn this song?" Yaw enquired of his little brother.

"No idea!"

On hearing his reply, everyone in the group burst into laughter!

"Quiet please!" Yaw cried out.

It took a while for silence to return.

"Okay, everyone pay attention." Yaw resumed. "I will sing the song three times through. Thereafter, you will sing after me. Is that okay with everyone?"

"Yes, please!" they replied as if with one voice.

After practising the song for a while, Kofi turned to the group:

"Let us get going. We are going to visit each home. We shall not leave any home we visit until the residents present us something —money, biscuits or both!"

As they moved on, Kofi wondered if anyone in the homes they were visiting would be impressed by the not-well-rehearsed Christmas carol they were singing and give them anything in return.

A pleasant surprise awaited them in the first home they visited. The moment they stopped on the open compound of the home, all the residents stopped whatever they were doing and gathered around them to listen to their songs. Those who were familiar with the songs joined in.

After singing the festive songs a few times over, the group stopped singing and prepared to move to the next home.

An elderly woman, who appeared to be the head of the family, brought out a red container filled with biscuits and placed three pieces in the outstretched hands of each of the group.

From there, the group continued on to the next home. After about half an hour of moving from house to house singing Christmas songs and wishing the residents a "Merry Christmas", the group dispersed to their respective homes.

* * *

As Kofi approached the compound of their home, he could smell the savoury smell of the Christmas meal being prepared by his mother.

"I am looking forward to a good meal!" Kofi told his two brothers walking beside him.

"Mother told me, she is cooking only one chicken. That is not very promising."

"Why?" Kofi enquired.

"Kofi, you are young so cannot remember. Last year mother cooked only a single chicken at Christmas. In the end, we received only small chunks of chicken to enjoy."

"I hope that is not the case this year," said Kofi.

"Well, let's wait and see."

After about three hours of work by their mother, the main Christmas meal was ready to be served. As to be expected, the meal for the occasion was fufu, which is the most popular meal in Kofi's culture. For those who are not familiar with fufu meal, here is a brief description:

The meal of fufu has two main components: the fufu dough and the soup to go with it. The ingredients needed for the fufu dough are boiled plantain and cassava.

The boiled plantain and cassava are pounded in a wooden mortar into a thick, sticky dough.

The unique thing about fufu is that one does not have to chew it; instead, one has to 'cut' a small lump with the fingers, dip the piece into the soup, place it on the tongue and swallow it.

In Kofi's culture, especially among those who live in small towns and villages such as Kookookrom, it is customary to share the main Christmas meal with relatives, friends and neighbours.

One does not invite such individuals into the home to eat from the same table. Instead one sends them portions of the meal by way of covered food bowls The duty falls on the children in the home to carry the food on their heads to those intended. Usually children above the age of six years are deemed big enough to assumed this role.

Amma Dede, Kofi's mother, is big-hearted. Instead of sharing the Christmas meals with only relatives, neighbours and close friends, it was her custom to share the meal with almost every household in the settlement!

"Take this portion to Family So-and-So. Hold on tightly to the bowl. Don't look left or right. Instead look straight so you don't fall over and spill the food," she instructed Yaw and Kwaku who she sent on errands to distribute the Christmas meals to other residents of the community.

Lucky Kofi! He did not have to take part in the task of carrying food to other members of the community. As already stated, children below the age of six were not considered big enough for the assignment.

When Yaw returned home from his fourth errand, he turned to his mother and began:

"Hey, Mama, we seem to be sharing our meal with the whole village. I am afraid there is not going to be any chicken meat left for us to enjoy!"

"We have been waiting all year long for the opportunity to enjoy our favourite meals only to feel short-changed!" Kwaku joined in.

"Don't worry, boys, there will be enough meat for everyone."

"I am not convinced!" That was Yaw.

"Why not?"

"I can see for myself; there is almost no more meat left in the soup bowl!"

"Don't worry!" Amma Dede still sought to reassure her boys.

"Why shouldn't I worry?" Kwaku still didn't sound convinced.

"It is not a one-way street; we are sharing with others. Others will also share with us."

"What happens if no one thinks about us?" Yaw wanted to know.

"Don't worry. All will be fine!" their mother continued to reassure them.

"That is exactly what you told me last year. We may indeed receive food from some of our neighbours. The question worth considering is: will what we receive be enough to compensate for what we have given out?"

Yaw and Kwaku were indeed right. After sharing their food with almost everyone in the village, they received food from only a couple of them in return.

In the end Kofi was assigned only a small piece of chicken liver.

"Take it, it is soft and delicious, you will really enjoy it."

"Is that all that is left for me?" he enquired.

"Yes, are you not happy?"

"I thought I would receive a big chunk of meat." he replied, looking disappointed.

"Don't be disappointed, my dear. Christmas is all about sharing. We shared lovingly with the rest of our community." Amma Dede tried to console the youngest member of the family.

"But we didn't receive as much as we gave out. That is not fair!" Yaw joined in the conversation.

"Never mind."

"No, I feel downhearted. I have waited the whole year for the opportunity to enjoy a good portion of chicken meat, only to feel let down!"

"Me too!" said Kwaku, in a sad voice.

"Hey, everyone! Christmas is a time of peace and joy. Stop arguing with your mother!" Kwabena Baah, reminded everyone.

* * *

The day was gradually drawing to a close. The bright African sun had disappeared from the skies. Darkness was drawing near. Soon Kofi would return to bed.

Though he would have wished for a far bigger chunk of chicken meat to enjoy, on the whole he was pleased with his first real Christmas experience.

In particular, he was proud of his new piece of ntama cloth. He would have wished his parents were in the position to buy him a pair of shoes as well. He was not disappointed however. Why should he be disappointed when he was aware he was not the only child of his parents who had to go about barefooted.

As he lay in bed, Kofi looked forward already to the next Christmas. Would his parents be in a good enough position to replace the ntama he had just received? He could only hope and pray they would. Soon Kofi was overtaken by sleep.

Oh Kofi! He might have carried the thoughts of Christmas into his sleep. Deep in the night, Yaw was suddenly awakened by a loud scream of: "Buronya aba, afe nhyia pa oo!"

As Yaw looked around half-asleep, wondering where the sound came from, he heard another cry of: "Buronya aba, afe nhyia pa oo!" He did not have to guess where it came from—it was from Kofi!

"Hey, shut up, boy, and don't disturb our sleep! Christmas is over!" Yaw shouted into his ears.

Kofi did not respond. Instead, Yaw could only hear the loud snores coming from his youngest brother. Despite these snores, Yaw was soon lost in sleep.

* * *

CHAPTER 4

On waking up the next morning Amma Dede was surprised to realise that none of her boys was awake. That was unusual, especially in the case of Kwaku.

She decided to open the door to go and check on them. On opening their door, she noticed all three of them were still fast asleep.

"Hey, boys, it is morning, get up everyone." she called out.

Initially none of them responded. After shouting aloud a second time, she managed to awaken them.

"Is everyone okay?" she enquired.

"Yes, indeed." Yaw and Kwaku replied as if with one voice.

"What about you, Kofi? Are you okay?"

"Yes, Mama. I wish you a Merry Christmas!"

"Don't wish Mama 'Merry Christmas'! Christmas is over!" Yaw pointed out.

"Christmas is over? Really?" Kofi enquired, looking surprised.

"Yes, of course," said Yaw.

"Ouch! I thought today too was Christmas!"

"No, it is over, boy!" Amma Dede pointed out to her little boy.

"So, Mama, how many days to go until the next Christmas?"

"Hey, Kofi shut up!" Kwaku shouted. "We just celebrated Christmas. You are not going to spend the next several months annoying us with never-ending questions about next Christmas, okay!"

"Okay, I promise."

"Sure?" Amma Dede appeared not convinced.

"Yes, Mama, I will certainly do that!"

One can only hope, along with the rest of Kofi's family, that he does indeed keep his word and not keep on troubling them by waking up each day with questions as to when to expect the next Christmas!

Look out for more exciting stories about Kofi Mensah, the little boy growing up in the little village of Kookookrom.

* * *

Glossary

Angel

A spiritual being believed to be a messenger from God. Usually shown wearing a white dress, wings on its back and a golden halo on its head.

Baby Jesus

Jesus is the son of God.

Bethlehem

Birthplace of Baby Jesus.

Boxing Day

26 December (the day after Christmas Day).

Buronya

Twi word for Christmas.

Cassava

The root of a cassava tree. Used to make flour.

Chicken meal	A meal of fufu balls with chicken soup eaten on 26 December, Boxing Day.
Christmas	Christmas is a festival to mark the birth of Baby Jesus in a little town called Bethlehem many years ago.
Christmas Day	25 December.
Christmas tree	A tree put up in a home at Christmas and decorated with sweets.
Cocoa	Also known as cacao. Used to make chocolate.
Favouritism	Treating one person better than the other.

Fufu dough   Meal made of boiled plantain and cassava.

Ghana   A country in West Africa.

Kerosene   A type of fuel, also known as paraffin, used in lamps and for heating in homes without electricity.

Kofi   Boy's name, meaning born on a Friday.

Kookookrom   Name of Kofi's village, meaning Cocoa Settlement.

Kaba   Girl's blouse.

Machete   Broad-bladed tool like an axe used in farming or as a weapon.

Makokrom	Nearest big town to Kookookrom. Means Pepper Settlement.
Measuring tape	A ruler made of clothing for measuring material.
Mensah	If parents give birth to a boy, to be followed directly by a boy and yet another boy, the third boy is called Mensah.
Mortar	A cup-shaped bowl in which ingredients are ground or mashed up.
Ntama cloth	An African wax print fabric used for making clothes.
Palm branches	Branches from the palm tree.

Plantain   Like a green banana.
                Used as a cooked
                vegetable.

Pastor   Minister in a church.

Tailor   A person who makes
                clothes out of material.

New Year   1 January.

ABOUT THE AUTHOR

Dr. Robert Peprah-Gyamfi grew up in Mpintimpi, a little village in Ghana, West Africa.

He faced many challenges growing up in that impoverished village.

Despite the challenging living conditions he faced growing up in that impoverished village, he later made it to the Hannover Medical School in Germany, where he qualified as a doctor in 1992.

Robert now works part -time as a doctor and spends the rest of his time writing. Indeed, he has been a passionate storyteller from a young age. He started his first novel as a teenager, but could not however finish his work due to lack of resources.

Robert, who regards himself as citizen of the Global Village, is currently resident in the UK.

To connect with him please visit:
www.kiddykiddybooks.com

www.ingramcontent.com/pod-product-compliance
Lightning Source LLC
Chambersburg PA
CBHW060115050426
42448CB00010B/1878